Full of Ears and Eyes Am I

poems by

Lauren Suchenski

Finishing Line Press
Georgetown, Kentucky

Full of Ears and Eyes Am I

To my son

Copyright © 2017 by Lauren Suchenski
ISBN 978-1-63534-243-7 First Edition
All rights reserved under International and Pan-American Copyright Conventions. No part of this book may be reproduced in any manner whatsoever without written permission from the publisher, except in the case of brief quotations embodied in critical articles and reviews.

ACKNOWLEDGMENTS

Publisher: Leah Maines

Editor: Christen Kincaid

Cover Art: Lauren Suchenski

Author Photo: Ryan T. Gingo, AFTEM LLC

Cover Design: Elizabeth Maines McCleavy

Printed in the USA on acid-free paper.
Order online: www.finishinglinepress.com
also available on amazon.com

Author inquiries and mail orders:
Finishing Line Press
P. O. Box 1626
Georgetown, Kentucky 40324
U. S. A.

Table of Contents

How does the present moment bleed into all forms 1
Fire heart, winter eyes 2
Perhaps the biggest reason to not grow old 3
There is cyber 4
I could trace the lines 5
Silent night sweet angel sounds 6
The wind belays me 7
A letter to the center of the universe: 9
Those who saw 10
Gently tap me out 11
Sometimes mother tells me stories 12
Hope 13
Thank you for this day 14
Consonants and vowels and places in between 15
I took a lap 16
Duck duck goose goose 17
Full of ears and eyes 18
And I'm not coming back 19
So white, wild 20
I have a set 21
Subsets 22
Just glow, she said 23
And glory glory to the word 24
Docu/ment 25
Find me here 26
And every blade of sunlight dreaming 27
I remember splatters of rain 28
I woke up to April 29

How does the present moment bleed into all forms

how does the present moment bleed into all forms
collapse into a puddle in the corner
whisk its way through silent reveries
and find itself dancing on the way home
with a thousand tangled webs spinning in its wake
how does the myriad face of a moving woman
belong to anything but time
anything but race and space and circus tents
all matters of remnants romancing themselves back
to the source
to the moment of momentous questionlessness
to that place where space contains
all of the spaces—empty and between
where little lives splay out like fingers,
play remembered chords
and sing old songs
not written yet

Fire heart, winter eyes

fire heart, winter eyes
moonbeam structure of the clouds
July you are always ticking inside my skin
churning for a way to burn out

life motion, love ripple
Time me to the tune of tinkling wonder

have I wondered enough
about the wandering of the wind?
have I longed deeply enough
for the long shadows of dusk
and have the curtain rod couplets of the dawn
brushed back my eyes enough
to see the light? To swallow it? To shed it without fear?
to shape my lowly hands with the shadow of the day?
have I tilted enough light into my bones yet?
or must I keep dragging myself towards that sun
like a pilgrim?

make this earth a mecca—I will lie down and worship its swollen hands
hold me, dear ground
and let me know
July is neverending

Perhaps the biggest reason to not grow old

Perhaps the biggest reason to not grow old
is that helpless way
that time begins to lose its meaning

that clichéd way that time speeds up
and silts out of the slits in your hands—
the weighted humidity that simmers
around those youthful memories
and grows thicker with insatiable power
while the present presence of your
already passing present
just slides around the surface of your skin

the way that mystery of taste cannot be replicated
once it has been consumed

There is cyber

there is cyber in my soul
there is rough and tumble in my roll
there are iron clad feet under my lipid languid legs
the shelter of my slithering cold cracked creaks and crags
my crinkled bony body
my sacred swelling skinsags
this is the dirt in my dwelling
this is the pound of flesh hanging onto my mossy mountain of moldy electrons

electronic tectonic plates pulse under my positions
and treasured tongues of tough leather are thick inside my museum of mouths

this is the way my flesh has frozen,
This is the shape I have shouldered
for a sum of momentous moments.
this is the track of time tensing inside my trickling-tripling-tenuous threads
all the little strings strung together

tied together like shoelaces, I am

slammed together like little bangs of the big bang
like little cosms of the cosmic microcosm
like little, little, littler and littlest.
that's how big.
that's how small this bundle of skin wants to be.
and is.

I could trace the lines

I could trace the lines
like a scar on the earth—
the places where the ground beneath our feet
got thinner and thinner

you can see the map stretched across time
the bedazzlement, the disillusionment,
the falling and folding and all the places
where tiny cracks collected

gravity pressed down on us
time—the erosion of all things beautiful and young
wind was a force
but mostly my tongue
my misinterpretation of what it was to share

you could chalk it up to signals firing
in the wrong direction
blame the brain
those nonsense neurons that refused to work with
the rest.
If you blame the brain it feels better

Silent night sweet angel sounds

silent night sweet angel sounds
sweet breath of baby's warmth
soft twilight dims the lucid taste
of moments far too present, far too honest and complete
someone's lost and listening
someone's 10 feet deep and ten stories tall
in the tallest stories ever told
someone's wild and free
and someone's growing fast
someone's lungs come galloping back
from the lifelong task of breathing
to drink from the wallowing willow—
the tune of laughter that sings through
the earth's body
the one last light whispering—
be born, be born, at last,
be born.

The wind belays me

The wind belays me
down through the weight of the light
the trust of the pathways of rain
the smell of the peach trees at dusk
and the winter of my summer's disillusion
now I swell now I swim
now I find my footing at last at last
what luck
what lady feet have tossed me under this tree
what swells of sunrise have galloped me apace
to the sweltering sensation of spring that blossoms through my brain
that sings in the grain
and twists up the sane
to the insanity of love
and the lust of the summer
all about and all above and all beside
the sycamore tree.
the scintillating softness of your perfect wide hot glance
the sun, the romance
and the cherry tree listening next door
the hurry to dissolve, to evaporate
and the absolution to give yourself away
to the sun, to the moon
to the everlasting drill of thoughtless rain
to the moment to the moment
to the endless july still tasting
a wand-less wordless window into wind
a piece of a piece of a presence
of a dissolving atmosphere
filling up perpetually
with a hatful of rain
and three right brains
tuned in the timeless trust
of tree on earth.

the me, the you and everything in the breeze.
nothing and nonsense and please.
here comes the river, here comes the river, here comes the presence at last.

A letter to the center of the universe:

To whom it may concern at the middle of the middle,

I demand a refund.
I demand a demonstration of what this nation stands for
I demand a re-do, a reply to the thousands of unanswered
questions I have thrown into the atmosphere.

I do not ask for much, I do not ask for many
but I ask for it all and I ask for plenty
I ask for things material, immaterial and imaginary
I ask for release from the boldly branded bonds to time
you so kindly shackled me to
I request a bigger salary, a higher chair, another dish
another taste, a long watery embrace of the mother who made me
I request a window seat. Some place where for just the briefest of moments
I can finally gaze upon the silence of the slice of this universe we call life
to see my own cell among the surface of the pond
drifting, dissolving, evolving and then finally forming once more, at last
ready to rain, once again free from brain.

Cordially yours,

Those who saw

those who saw the end of the world were not invited to return.
those tiny sprawling few who tasted the filament of the fine film of the edge
could only gasp backwards at a world they had not yet begun to see.

stars collapsing in on themselves from heavy grace
fell through decades of ancient space-breath
folded napkins blowing in the wind affixed themselves permanently to the
landscape of a frozen silence

those who felt the sapphire silence of the center
bubbling around them like cannon fire and courage
no longer felt the bite, the know, the claw of human ignition

those who saw
say they lifted up, gathered about, reared back, roared through
dissolved and better-ed and burned. sat like ash at the whirlpool of meteoric
mystery
blew through the universe like chunks of falling atmosphere
hovered through the timeless
and named themselves
something too far, too fast, too free to be followed.

Gently tap me out

Gently tap me out.
Tumble my burns and ashes into the whirlpool
of light we all hunt for.
Gently, ever so gently,
let it be me I return to.

Swallow me whole, season of summer—
let these amber drops of golden wanting
wish me down the spiral staircase

up through the hungry roots, past the furrowing
browns of trunks of tireless trees

let me spurn myself into a photosynthesizing mythical-izing
spit-fire capsizing master of light
let me get a taste of that light with you, oh brother blade.
let me get a taste of that light.

Gently, wrestle me out.
tip my soul from my bones
and let me grow with the green things
and the legions of dirt
let me surround myself with soil
and splay out into the reach of the sky

let me, let me, let me
curl my own toes into the burrowing of buried browns
and blacks

soil-rich with oxygen, let me breathe full breaths of
borrowed time. Gently, tap me out.
and follow me down this path of ever-ending
never-failing, firmly-rooted floating;

the air and everything in it full of sound and bacteria.

Sometimes mother tells me stories

sometimes mother tells me stories.
sometimes mother braids my hair—
grass-seed-feed and long-legged-goose-songs
sometimes mother leads me to water, sometimes mother leads me to shelter.
always, mother sings her silent dance.

sometimes father invents the sky
sometimes brother tramples the forest
sometimes sister pulls the apron of the sky
over the skirt legs of the sea.
sometimes hurricane sun swallows sand.
always, mother sings her silent dance.

used to be, people knew when family went missing
used to be, shadowed sunsets always sunk
but now and then and nowadays,
days go drifting through your hands

putty-silk and satin-gold—days go drifting through your hands

some wash up and some wash out,
some grow back and some grow in,
some turn time like wheels of grain, some burn brains
like ash and ember
some leave earth to tick and tock
but always mother sings her silent dance.

Hope

Hope
or something like it
dangles from a chain around your neck
playing carefully with the light
and the reverberations of sound on the wall

love, or something we once tucked
in the back pocket of our jeans
coming smothering towards us
basking and asking for nothing in return
but a drop of our midnight eyes to remain
transfixed in the moment forever.

well that forever was a long time past
and the past keeps passing by
to tell me the time, to alert me of the way the wind
keeps washing me side to side
and to give me firm enough ground to stand on
that i might begin to glimpse the future.

barreling down on three tracks and twelve trains,
the future is coming. silent and heaving
and always leaving nothing behind
but salt and skin and sweat

and when it meets me, when it greets me
and takes me by the hand
shakes me up and down and startles me into submission
I think I'll board that train—
ride it to the dust of the dusk
and let it swallow me whole.

Thank you for this day

thank you for this day
and the miles of moments that
litter the way from here to there
and there to there and back again.

thank you for this breath
and the sudden thrill of wings on air;
the violent upswing of sunlight on
streams of summer heat

thank you for this wild unkempt
Circle
which draws me in, which draws me in
which shows me the sound of July
points me towards the water
and gives me back my swimming spine.

Consonants and vowels and places in between

consonants and vowels and places in between
longing, longing, I am a longing machine
a long, draped memory of a space
I used to fill

silence, silence I am a pitter patter machine
a drumming voice of cataclysmic choice
the size of sounds I never knew
how to pronounce

tunnel, tunnel I am always reaching
through the underside
of a great bottomless barrel of light
I am always spinning on my head—
Looking up at last to find my name
written on the roof of my mouth
covered in corners of consonants, vowels,
and reverberations of what it feels like
to feel like what it is
to be named.

I took a lap

I took a lap around the rings of Saturn this morning
just to move my legs—to jolt my sense of sensation
to feel the turbulent curvature of a circle around the tips of my toes
turning like a perfect demonstration of a square

I felt the radioactive kiss of space
the utter, outer, open space of spacelessness
the breathless quality of quantitative space dust
and the space between myself and the self that I could reach

I felt the Zeno paradox closing around my ankles
the turpentine, turquoise turtle and the fumbling stripes of Apollo
that rumbled ahead and behind me, constantly looping me
in a test of speed and grace
I felt
the wilderness of rain and all the excuses the sun made to itself
calling itself Light
calling itself light

Duck duck goose goose

duck duck goose goose
gallop green gaseous gorgeous word word whirling
twirling little drops of decadence into the fraction of your firmament
we're going to multiply with the reciprocal,
with the receiving end of a dividing line
with the simplification of a truly sublime circumference—
that big earth waist. wading in deep
to the cosmic waters of your recycled sum.
the sum of all the sun's light does not equal
the number of numbers left waddling in the words.
convert it into a fraction of its former life and freeze it.
repeat, release, repackage,
rehash and reverberate our sacred stories through the sterile strainer
of our soundcollage named science and force it into the
little fermented fragmented of
an integer. an integral part of integrating
into the interdependency of the idiosyncracy
of spacetime named now.

Full of ears and eyes

full of ears and eyes and heads and toes am I
full of fulls and empties
dredges of paint cans
and highway hands

full of ears and eyes am I
lost empires of empirical data
dainty delicious deliveries of destinies
and strange subtle tunes of saccharine sentimentality

this poem is always about nothing,
this poem that I write over and over
just the words—no hues, no fears, no weary wonderballs
this is the poem/this is the poem I am always writing
the sound of my sorrowshoes slicing against pavement
the memory of swollen words uttering faceless expressions
the sagging sack of surrendered silence
and then there—that word beyond words
that sound inside the star.

When the entire sky is so full of star-sentience that we can barely make out sentences—
just pitter patter poem fragments of words
or half uttered syllables
or barely edible
letter litters
lingering
up and
down
streets,sidewalks,forests,corporate-complexes and mountains

Then I'll come back. Then I'll come back, I
Promise.

And I'm not coming back

And I'm not coming back she said
she heaved, she sighed, she slid the silver moon over the bespeckled eyes of bedraggled dragon hearts
of caustic causation and plastic plausibility
of things that form and formulate
of words that reel and reveal
of times that tuck and turn and twist and worlds that measure fire and water
in terms of air and earth
and all the boundless energies of energetic enigmas
swallowing tubular tentacles of truth
for breakfast, lunch, dinner, supper and supposition

So white, wild

so white, wild and whimsical
so weird, worldly and wordy
big orange cabbage collections of directions
I can cook and I can clean but all that needs to be done
is more doing, less seeing, more seething—
more teething on the cold watery sweat of the sun.

the driplets and droplets of drooping old sun
segway into the sequential square (the radiant stare of that big blinking eye)
past the diving post of postulation named time. named rhyme. named I am
forsooth, for tooth for ache for breaking brown light on the edged side of the universe

this is a poem called pride. this is a quantum leap through
cracks in time, my mind and my mattergoop.
this is the flame of the land and the
slit of the sound parade
that named itself
nameless.

this is the form of being formed as a little jagged mouth twirling into the universe.

I have a set

I have a set, it's the largest set there is

there's no largest set, for example.

is equal to, is equal to
is equal to the equator, floating above your head.
our one to three, one through three, two, too too much to free again.
our mathmap mad mask. our blank bank of (our set not on the list)
setting out to start, to restart. I keep setting out to set things in place, to place things in motion
to motivate my own movementlessness.

Subsets

subsets are,
for example,
know how to,
even with nothing in it,
even with everything in it,
all the subsets of the powersets, set it time settling into the set of all subsets.
so we just list them all?
we just listlessly listen to the lists of all the Capital letters letting go
isn't there also the set that has nothing in it?
this is the equation
this is the hurricane nation. this is the hero and
the norwegian zero.

there are more real numbers than integers, then the integration of interest
and the rise and fall of the natural history of naturalism (the theory is
there are more real numbers than natural numbers)
it's true, but it's really about infinite sets.
that's what it's used for.

but that's just an example.

Just glow, she said

just glow, she said.
she laid her head down to rest
laid the rest down to resist and began to pull
to snap, to slice and tear all sense asunder.

just know, she said
there is nothing in this nowhere that doesn't belong
to you—not at least in part, in particle or participle.
there is nothing here to be known that is not unspeakable.

i said, i said.
nowhere can you find me—
i am hiding in the place where no words can reach
can hum, can teach
i am sliding into sounds and i am curving into creation
cracking, creaking and absorbing
i am somewhat somewhere always now
and no one no where can know how.

just wait, she said.
she said all the world will sit in your head
will rewrite just at the end, at the top, at the beginning
flip on its toes and turn on the edges
lead you through sense to the great drumming beat
to the place without feet, without hands, without heat
and then you'll know then what you cannot know now
how to how, when to when, and more than could
ever be said.

And glory glory to the word

and glory glory to the word
named grass

to the long opalescent tracks of sunset that streak across
your ribs, your bones and all the grazing places
where your soul must hide

glory glory to the star called sun
and all its devastating bliss that wants to
ignite the space no longer stuck in time

the world has wings and the world has aching breaking backbones
the world echoes on and the world collapses in

i sit at the center and watch my center swirl inwards
and my innards curve outwards and upwards
through the mild architecture of my form—
final, resolute and resplendent.

glory glory to the gore and gutter of your core
to the rage and sputter of your lungs
that keep forcing syllables into words and sentences into stories
and something involving sense into the great mass
of momentous matter you call man.

Docu/ment

Docu-ment
is that what you meant?
to document my life—swollen guitar strings
and all the hairs in my spine?

is that what you meant?
curled toe prints and unkempt wax stains (I dropped the burning candle
on the table—the heat was
just enough to
stay)

Doc
tor? Or
.docx? .Doc
fix me, fix me,
my followers only follow me
so far
my memories only linger so fontlessly
my faces only glare back at me with so many filterless fantasies

Doc, you meant
to heal,
you meant to seal the edges, seep up the sutures,
step up the sanctity, surround yourself with sanity
and remain sanitary. remain sanitary.
safe. and sound.
and seen.

Find me here

Find me here where I am waiting

This patch of land still grazing—
still wading
deep into the bosom of the water

Still suckling—wide-eyed and planet-sized
map-born and wind-less.
Find me here where I am young, old and fruitful
Where I am no more than the veins of a river
pouring oxygen into the trill of a watershed

Find me here; I am walking
I am walking
I am no man but the nomad I once was.
I am no more sure-footed than the feet I once carved
out of maps (or something that directed me
to the present moment)

And every blade of sunlight dreaming

and every blade of sunlight dreaming
is a disc of holy sound
a record skipping on repeat
a thousand silences murmured incomplete

and every wild wind
tapping at my window
can see the way the world now shapes
around my waist, my weeds, my wonder

all the thunder and all the courage
of a sinking blade of sunlight dreaming
is a fired-rage of heartened glass
precipitating rain. (rain and sun and something in between)

rhythm beats like hungry teeth
that chatter in the arctic dawn
bridgeless gaps of sky and sea keep stretching soundlessly
but I am here, and I am drenched
in blades of sunlight streaming.

I remember splatters of rain

I remember splatters of rain
across your bones

and the way the water of your eyes
felt like silence

I remember 19 thousand words I never said
and a couple or three I never should have

I remember your raw elephant tusk of a heart
piercing wildly through the fumbling of the night
and a swollen promise the world would not let us keep

I remember stones inside my feet;
courage inside my spine; and the erect disdain
for anything resembling honesty

I remember trainwrecks
or I remember you

but never at the same time
can I splice them into one image

Split-frame
that's how my heart keeps you alive.

I woke up to April

I woke up to April

pressing down on my ribcage with a smile
tucking me into the season
and giving me all the wrong reasons to breathe.
I woke up never having seen March
and wondering where the ground
had evaporated to

I watched the water of this world
sift sweetly and sacredly through the silt of the soil
and it came to pass that all that seemed yellow
was now green

I woke up from a dreamless wonder
wandering and weary from the imposition
and the position of my skin against the wind

I woke up and kept waking up
kept breathing through my silly putty nostrils
kept sinking through the holes in the ozone
kept wishing for the world to return to me

such a tiny sweet curl this day gave me
wrapped behind my ear
waiting to listen to the Spring
waiting to listen to the world wake up

Lauren Suchenski has a difficult relationship with punctuation and currently lives in Yardley, PA. She was nominated for the Pushcart Prize in 2015 and adores her little boy. You can find more of her writing on Instagram @lauren_suchenski or on Twitter @laurensuchenski.

www.ingramcontent.com/pod-product-compliance
Lightning Source LLC
LaVergne TN
LVHW041511070426
835507LV00012B/1501